Thoor Ballylee

1. Thoor Ballylee, c. 1926.

Mary Hanley & Liam Miller

Thoor Ballylee
home of William Butler Yeats

with a foreword by T. R. Henn

Colin Smythe

First published by The Dolmen Press, Dublin, in June 1965.
Second edition, revised: 1977, reprinted 1984.
Text layout by Liam Miller.

Third edition, with additional illustrations,
published in Great Britain in 1995
by Colin Smythe Limited, Gerrards Cross, Buckinghamshire

This paper is a development of a lecture delivered by Mary
Hanley to the Kiltartan Society at Coole Park on 19 June
1961, rearranged with additional matter by Liam Miller.

ISBN 0-85105-511-7

Printed in Great Britain

Illustrations

1. Thoor Ballylee, c. 1926 — *frontis*

2. Sketch by Lady Gregory, dated 14 August 1895 — *page 6*

3. Map of Ballylee and district — 8

4. Thoor Ballylee before reconstruction — 12

5. Plans of Thoor Ballylee as reconstructed — 14

6. Drawing of a table by Professor William A. Scott, 1918 — 17

7. Thoor Ballylee: The dining room, 1926 — 19

8. Thoor Ballylee: The bedroom, 1926 — 21

9. Thoor Ballylee: The living room, 1926 — 22

10. Thoor Ballylee: Fireplace in the living room, 1926 — 22

11. Cover design by T. Sturge Moore for *The Tower*, 1928 — 24

12. The inscription carved at Thoor Ballylee — 25

13. W. B. Yeats and his children at Ballylee, 1926 — 27

14. The thatching of the cottage, 1964 — 28

15. Thoor Ballylee, from the vegetable garden, c. 1926 — 29

16. Sketches by Lady Gregory, 14 August 1895 — 30

Plates 2 and 17, drawn by Lady Gregory on 14 August 1895, are reproduced by permission of Anne de Winton and Catherine Kennedy. Plates 7, 8, 9, 10, 13 and possibly 1 and 15 are from photographs taken by Mr. Thomas Haynes on a visit to Thoor Ballylee in 1926. Plate 14 is from a photograph by Bord Failte. Plate 15 is reproduced by permission of Anne Yeats.

2. Sketch by Lady Gregory, dated 14 August 1895.

Foreword

Thoor Ballylee was Yeats's monument and symbol; in both aspects it had multiple significance. It satisfied his desire for a rooted place in a known countryside, not far from Coole and his life-long friend Lady Gregory. To live in a Tower completed, perhaps, his alignment with a tradition of cultivated aristocracy which he had envied and a leisured peace which he had enjoyed. Its long and violent history, the Norman keep protecting the cottages that adjoined it, its association with the beautiful Mary Hynes, the healing properties of the 'mill,' the mystery and emblem of the river that vanished underground; these were facets which satisfied his instinct for the dramatic in history, warfare, society.

But there were many related thoughts. There were the associations with Shelley and Milton, and with Samuel Palmer's engravings for *Il Penseroso*: beyond that, thoughts beyond number of the ascent to wisdom by the winding stair. The crumbling battlements might stand for the broken parapets of Europe; the raids during the Troubles no more than a repetition of the Tower's part in older wars. Many aspects of the wildlife about it, and the stony pastures beside, were pressed to serve as emblems: otter, moorhen, heron, trout; the trees that stood against the gales coming in from the Atlantic; the thorn of the crags; butterflies and moths came to the window, to recall those classical emblems; bees, to symbolize co-operation and sweetness, that came to the crevices of the ruined masonry to give in the poem called 'The Stare's Nest by My Window' a final judgement on the Irish dilemma:

> We had fed the heart on fantasies,
> The heart's grown brutal from the fare;
> More substance in our enmities
> Than in our love; O honey-bees,
> Come build in the empty house of the stare.[1]

These, and many other aspects of the Tower, served Yeats. By 1958 it was falling to ruin once again, though with one added symbol which would have pleased the poet: a plough and a cart stood stored in the lower room. Coole, which might have served as a superb monument to the whole movement, was destroyed out of ignorance and lack of imagination to make 'mean roof-trees . . . the sturdier for its fall.'[2]

The Tower has been saved by The Kiltartan Society, and above all by the energy and pertinacity of its President, Mrs. Mary Hanley, without whom nothing of this great record would have come to pass. Our debt to the Society and to her is immeasurable.

T. R. HENN   April 1965

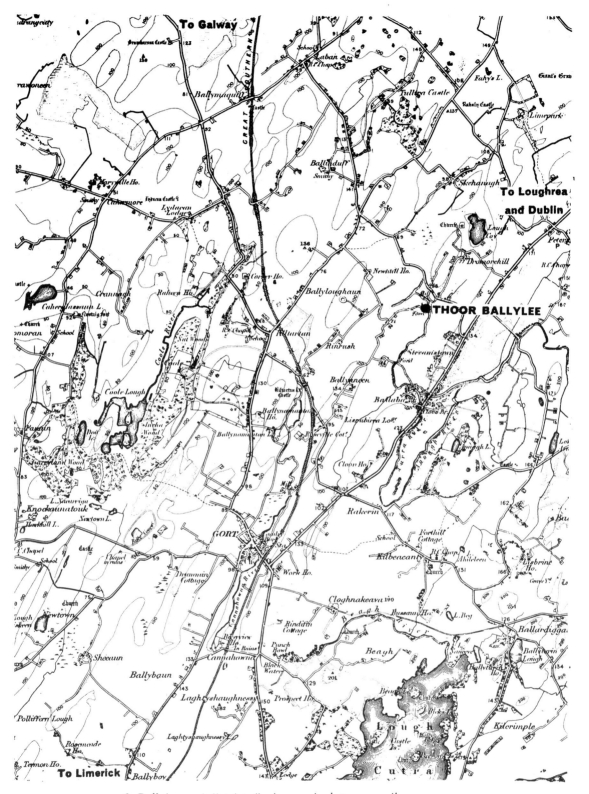

3. Ballylee and district. Scale: one inch to one mile.
Based on the Ordnance Survey by permission of the Government (Permit No. 524).

Thoor Ballylee

The Norman Family de Burgo, or Burke, were extensive landowners in the district around Kilmacduagh on the borders of Counties Clare and Galway, and during the thirteenth and fourteenth centuries their family erected thirty-two fortified residences, 'castles,' 'keeps' or 'towers' in this district. The de Burgos eventually so outgrew the old Gaelic territorial lords both in number and in influence that by the first half of the seventeenth century they had become masters of almost half the territory known as *Hy Fiachrach Aidhne*. An account, dated 1606, claims that at that time there were more able-bodied men named Burke than there were of any other name in Europe and that these Burkes were most numerous in the district around Gort in County Galway.

The castles or towers built by the Burkes can be traced today at Loughrea, Kilcornan, Kilcolgan, Dunkellin, Cloghcroke, St. Clerans, Mannin, Iser Kelly, Castletown, Ballyconnell, Ballyturin and at Ballylee, which is some three miles north-east of Gort. It was this last castle, 'Thoor Ballylee,' that the poet William Butler Yeats acquired and converted as his home in 1917. 'Two men have founded here,' he wrote in 'Meditations in time of Civil War'

> A man at arms . . .
> And I, that after me
> My bodily heirs may find,
> To exalt a lonely mind,
> Befitting emblems of adversity.[1]

Yeats liked to recall the old warriors who lived in Thoor Ballylee centuries before him, and he imagined them climbing the 'narrow winding stair' in their armour,

> Before that ruin came, for centuries,
> Rough men-at-arms, cross-gartered to the knees
> Or shod in iron, climbed the narrow stairs,
> And certain men-at-arms there were
> Whose images, in the Great Memory stored,
> Come with loud cry and panting breast
> To break upon a sleeper's rest
> While their great wooden dice beat on the board.[2]

Ballylee is situated in the Barony of Kiltartan which adjoins the Barony of Loughrea in County Galway. The Cloon river meanders through this low-lying, rolling countryside, dropping over a thirty-foot waterfall before it flows past Thoor Ballylee and afterwards disappearing into a subterranean passage on its way to enter the Atlantic Ocean which is about twenty miles westward. To the east the Slieve Aughty mountains dominate the landscape. Three miles west of Thoor Ballylee, the main road from Galway to Limerick runs from north to south and passes by Coole Park, the estate of Lady Gregory's family, and then through Gort, the market town of the district.

The local place-names, Laban, Kilbecanty, Cloon, and Kiltartan all figure largely in the setting of Lady Gregory's folk plays and the dialect she invented is popularly dubbed 'Kiltartan' after the last of these.

> My country is Kiltartan Cross,
> My countrymen Kiltartan's poor,[3]

Yeats wrote in 1919 in his poem commemorating the death of Lady Gregory's son, Robert, and from Kiltartan Cross a road branches. northeast from the main road and leads to Tulira Castle which was the home of the third founder of the Irish National Theatre, Edward Martyn.

The Booke of Connaught, 1585, lists Ballylee as Islandmore Castle, then in the possession of Edward Ulick de Burgo, who died there in 1597. In 1617 the castle is recorded as the property of Richard de Burgo, Earl of Clanrickarde. After the Reformation, the de Burgo family remained Catholic and during the seventeenth and eighteenth centuries the Penal Laws effectively destroyed the power, wealth and influence of the family. Their lands passed into the ownership of Protestant settlers in the area, the Persses, the Lamberts, the Martyns and the Gregorys. The de Burgos were virtually extinct in the area by the end of the nineteenth century, as is recorded by Monsignor Fahey in *The History and Antiquities of the Diocese of Kilmacduagh*, published in Dublin in 1893.

In the middle of the nineteenth century Ballylee was owned by James Colgan of Kilcolgan Castle. He leased Thoor Ballylee as a residence to his nephew, Patrick Spellman who was Master of the Workhouse at Loughrea. Patrick Spellman and his wife lived in the tower apartments and later built the adjoining cottage for the younger members of their family. The Spellmans were living at Thoor Ballylee when Yeats first visited there in 1896. Mrs. Spellman died there in 1902 and when the family gave up their occupancy, Thoor Ballylee became part of the estate of the Gregory family at Coole Park.

In the autumn of 1895 Yeats moved from his family home at Blenheim Road in Bedford Park, to share chambers with his friend Arthur Symons at Fountain Court in the Temple in London. During the following year the two friends decided to spend part of August and September on a walking tour in the West of Ireland. They visited Sligo and the Aran Islands where Yeats hoped to acquire local colour for his novel, *The Speckled Bird*, which he had promised to Bullen, his London publisher, who had paid him an advance. They stayed at Tulira Castle as guests of Edward Martyn and here Yeats was introduced to Lady Gregory. After Symons returned to London, Yeats spent some days as Lady Gregory's guest at Coole Park and during this, his first time in the area which was to be so significant in his life, he first came to Ballylee.

He recorded his first impressions of Ballylee in an essay, 'Dust hath closed Helen's eye,' which was first printed in *The Dome* in October 1899 and which he included in *The Celtic Twilight* when he revised and enlarged the book in 1902.

I have been lately to a little group of houses, not many enough to be called a village, in the barony of Kiltartan in County Galway, whose name, Ballylee, is known through all the west of Ireland. There is the old square castle, Ballylee, inhabited by a farmer and his wife, and a cottage where their daughter and their son-in-law live, and a little mill with an old miller, and old ash trees throwing green shadows upon a little river and great stepping-stones. I went there two or three times last year to talk to the miller about Biddy Early, a wise woman that lived in Clare some years ago, and about her saying "There is a cure for all evil between the two mill-wheels of Ballylee," and to find out from him or another whether she meant the moss between the running waters or some other herb. I have been there this summer and I shall be there again before it is autumn, because Mary Hynes, a beautiful woman whose name is still a wonder by turf fires, died there sixty years ago; for our feet would linger where beauty has lived its life of sorrow to make us understand that it is not of the world.[4]

Yeats was charmed by the thought of 'Mary Hynes, the shining flower of Ballylee,' who had been celebrated in the eighteenth century in verses by the Gaelic poet Raftery which Lady Gregory had translated under the title 'Raftery's praise of Mary Hynes' and which were printed at the Cuala Press in 1918 in her *Kiltartan Poetry Book*.

There is sweet air on the side of the hill, when you are looking down upon Ballylee; when you are walking in the valley picking nuts and blackberries, there is music of the birds in it and music of the Sidhe.

What is the worth of greatness till you have the light of the flower of the branch that is by your side? There is no good to deny it or to try and hide it; she is the sun in the heavens who wounded my heart.

There was no part in Ireland I did not travel, from the rivers to the tops of the mountains; to the edge of Lough Greine whose mouth is hidden, and I saw no beauty but was behind hers.

Her hair was shining and her brows were shining too; her face was like herself, her mouth pleasant and sweet; she is the pride and I give her the branch; she is the shining flower of Ballylee.

It is Mary Hynes, the calm and easy woman, has beauty in her mind and in her face. If a hundred clerks were gathered together, they could not write down a half of her ways.[5]

*

During the long and close association between Yeats and Lady Gregory from their first meeting in 1896 until her death in 1932, Yeats was a frequent visitor to Coole. He spent many summers there, writing his poems and plays and gradually he came to think that he should acquire a place for himself in the district. In 1916 the Congested Districts Board was in the process of acquiring part of the Gregory estates for redistribution among the people who were smallholders in the neighbourhood, and among the properties relinquished by the estate was Ballylee Castle, a property which comprised the tower, the two attached cottages, one of which was then in ruins, the walled garden and the grove of trees which faced the castle across the road.

4. Thoor Ballylee before reconstruction.

Yeats negotiated with the Board to purchase this property, which nobody else wanted, and during the winter of 1916 he concluded the transaction for an outright purchase price of £35. In a letter written to Olivia Shakespear on 8 November 1916 he already referred to the property as 'my castle.'[6] By 12 May of the following year he could write to his father

I came here to take over my Tower, Ballylee Castle. I shall make it habitable at no great expense and store there so many of my possessions that I shall be able to have less rooms in London. The Castle will be an economy, counting the capital I spend so much a year, and it is certainly a beautiful place. There are trout in the river under the window. Jack can come there when he wants Connaught people to paint.[7]

Three days later he wrote to Olivia Shakespear:

The castle is to be handed over to me tomorrow. The architect has been down and I know what I am going to do. The little cottage is to be repaired and extended so as to put in a quite comfortable and modern part-kitchen, bathroom, sitting room, three bedrooms. I am then to go on to the castle at my leisure. The cottage on the island will be arranged so as to give me privacy shutting me off from the road thus. [*Here follows a rough plan.*]
The cottage will make a kind of cloister and will be thatched. [*Here follows a rough sketch, marked* "very bad drawing".] This will give me a little garden shut in by these and by the river. The cottage will cost I believe £200. The old outhouses to supply the stonework. My idea is to keep the contrast between the mediaeval castle and the peasant's cottage. As I shall have the necessities in the cottage I can devote the castle to a couple of great rooms and for very little money.[8]

The conversion and adaptation of the property to his needs occupied much of Yeats's time during the summer of 1917. The Tower consisted of four floors with one room on each, connected by a spiral stone stairway built into the seven-foot thickness of the massive outer wall. Each floor had a window overlooking the river which flowed alongside. At the top there was a flat roof reached by a final steep flight of steps from the floor below. The cottage which the Spellmans had built was connected to the original entrance door of the Tower by a porch, which Yeats had extended to form an entrance to a second cottage which he had built behind, and parallel to the first. A walled garden adjoined the cottage and, across the road which passed Ballylee a grove of trees surrounded another plot of land on which a small outhouse was later built as a garage.

Yeats was in London during June, but returned to Coole Park early in July, having consulted his architect in Dublin, and decided to start work on the castle at once and leave the cottage until later.[9] To pay for the conversion he planned

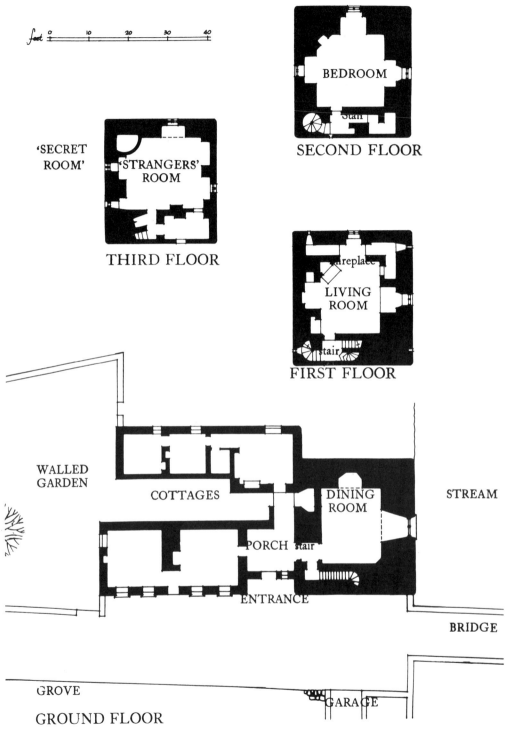

5. Plans of Thoor Ballylee as reconstructed.
From drawings made by Mr. Drmot O'Toole.

to give some lectures in Paris and probably in Milan — my old subjects — and shall earn enough to roof the castle.[10]

The architect, William A. Scott, Professor of Architecture at the National University of Ireland, prepared the working drawings and by August, when Yeats went to France, a local builder, Thomas Rafferty, had commenced work. The furniture for the Tower was made in Gort by a craftsman joiner, Patrick Connolly, after Professor Scott's designs, and the ironwork was also executed in Gort, at Burke's forge.

Lady Gregory was left in charge of the building operations during Yeats's absence in France and the letters he sent to her at this time show his concern for the work. He wrote to her on 12 August from Colleville sur Mer, where he was visiting Iseult Gonne,

Whatever happens there will be no immediate need of money, so please see that Raftery goes to work at Ballylee. I told him to put "shop shutters" on cottage but now I do not want him to put any kind of shutter without Scott's directions. When you need another £50 from me let me know.[11]

and again on 21 August,

Thanks for Raftery's estimate which is much what I thought it would be. I think it possible that Scott may decide it better not to wall up that door — I want him to decide. I have also asked him to decide about doors etc. If Raftery has got to wait he will have plenty to do on roof, walls etc., so Scott's advice will not be late.[12]

Yeats proposed marriage to Iseult Gonne and was refused by her during this visit. In September he returned to England and proposed to Miss George Hyde-Lees. They were married on 20 October. His marriage made the completion of his Irish home a matter of urgency to Yeats and he continued to ask Lady Gregory about the progress of the work at Ballylee. On 29 October he wrote,

Is Raftery at work on Ballylee? — if he is I will write to Gogarty and ask him to stir up Scott.[13]

In December the Yeatses planned a visit to Coole, to take place early in the following month, and a letter to Lady Gregory on 16 December reveals how marriage had brought a new order to his domestic life,

I wish you could see Woburn Buildings now — nothing changed in plan but little touches here and there, and my own bedroom (the old bathroom) with furniture of unpainted unpolished wood such as for years I have wished for. Then there is a dinner service of great purple plates for meat and various earthenware bowls for other purposes.[14]

The proposed visit to Coole was postponed from January because Yeats contracted influenza. Early in February Robert Gregory was killed in a war action, flying in Italy. The visit which had been deferred until Easter and for which Lady Gregory had offered them a house, was further postponed. Nevertheless, Yeats pressed on with the work at Ballylee, and reported to Lady Gregory on 22 February,

Raftery gets on slowly but fairly steadily with his work at Ballylee, and has just written that the rats are eating the thatch. Scott has asked for dimensions of fireplaces so evidently will send designs and the Castle has been cleaned out. It looks as if this Spring may see the roof on, but I don't want my wife to spend more money till she has seen the place.[15]

In May 1918 Yeats and his wife went to stay at Ballymantane House which Lady Gregory had loaned to them while work went on at Ballylee. Shortages of materials had slowed up the work, but Yeats found compensation in the fact that he could purchase old materials, beams, planks and stone, locally. By July he had definite hopes of moving into the Tower and wrote a letter, dated 23 July, to John Quinn, expressing this,

My dear Quinn, This letter is written in hope, that is to say, I hope it will be true a day or two after this letter reaches you, at the latest. We are surrounded with plans. This morning designs arrived from the drunken man of genius, Scott, for two beds. The war is improving the work, for, being unable to import anything, we have bought the whole contents of an old mill — great beams and three-inch planks, and old paving stones; and the local carpenter and mason and blacksmith are at work for us. On a great stone beside the front door will be inscribed these lines:

> I, the poet, William Yeats,
> With common sedge and broken slates
> And smithy work from the Gort forge,
> Restored this tower for my wife George;
> And on my heirs I lay a curse
> If they should alter for the worse,
> From fashion or an empty mind,
> What Raftery built and Scott designed.

Raftery is the local builder. . . .
I am making a setting for my old age, a place to influence lawless youth, with its severity and antiquity. If I had this tower when Joyce began I might have been of use, have got him to meet those who might have helped him.[16]

The optimism of this letter was not fulfilled and in September Yeats was still hoping to move into the castle, as a letter to Clement Shorter, written in that month shows:

We are hoping every day to get into our castle where we are, or it is, constantly looking after carpenters and the like. We shall live on the road like a

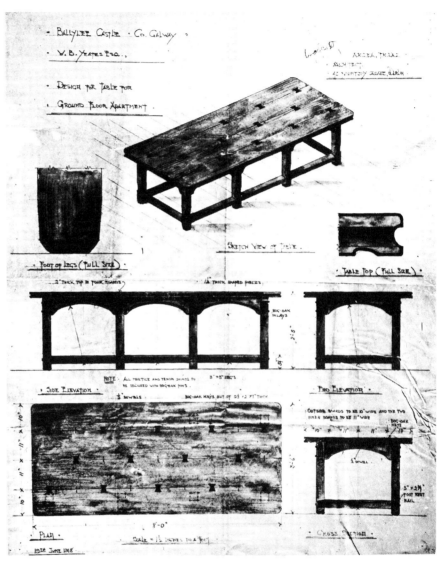

6. Drawing for a table by Professor William A. Scott, 1918.
The design was not executed.

country man, our white walled cottage with its border of flowers like any country cottage and then the gaunt castle. [*Here follows a sketch.*] All work — furniture and all — is being done by local labour. We have plenty of timber as we bought the hundred year old floors and beams of a mill.[17]

His poem, 'In Memory of Major Robert Gregory,' completed during that summer, reflects his hope :

Now that we're almost settled in our house
I'll name the friends that cannot sup with us
Beside a fire of turf in th' ancient tower,
And having talked to some late hour
Climb up the narrow winding stair to bed.[18]

*

By the summer of 1919 Yeats was in residence at Ballylee Castle and the extent to which his home was to become one of his most important symbols is indicated in 'A Prayer on going into my House':

God grant a blessing on this tower and cottage
And on my heirs, if all remain unspoiled,
No table or chair or stool not simple enough
For shepherd lads in Galilee; and grant
That I myself for portions of the year
May handle nothing and set eyes on nothing
But what the great and passionate have used
Throughout so many varying centuries. . . .[19]

And in 'My House' in the sequence of poems entitled 'Meditations in Time of Civil War' he described his home:

An ancient bridge, and a more ancient tower,
A farmhouse that is sheltered by its wall,
An acre of stony ground,
Where the symbolic rose can break in flower,
Old ragged elms, old thorns innumerable,
The sound of the rain or sound
Of every wind that blows;
The stilted water-hen
Crossing stream again
Scared by the splashing of a dozen cows;

A winding stair, a chamber arched with stone,
A grey stone fireplace with an open hearth,
A candle and written page.
Il Penseroso's Plantonist toiled on
In some like chamber, shadowing forth
How the daemonic rage
Imagined everything.
Benighted travellers
From markets and from fairs
Have seen his midnight candle glimmering.

Two men have founded here. A man-at-arms
Gathered a score of horse and spent his days
In this tumultuous spot,
Where through long wars and sudden night alarms
His dwindling score and he seemed castaways

Forgetting and forgot;
And I, that after me
My bodily heirs may find,
To exalt a lonely mind,
Befitting emblems of adversity.[20]

During the summer of 1919 the castle and life with his wife and his
daughter, who had been born earlier that year, made a centre for
Yeats's life, and the tower became more and more his 'monument
and symbol,' as he wrote in a letter to John Quinn on 11 July:

And would I mind if Sinn Fein took possession of my old tower here to store
arms in, or the young scholars from the school broke all the new windows?
I think my chief difficulty in accepting will be my tower, which needs another year's work under our own eyes before it is a fitting monument and
symbol, and my garden, which will need several years if it is to be green and
shady during my lifetime. Ballylee is a good house for a child to grow up in—
a place full of history and romance, with plenty to do every day.[21]

7. Thoor Ballylee: The dining room, 1926.

It was also a good place in which to write, as a letter to his father
on 16 July shows:

I am writing in the great ground floor of the castle — pleasantest room I have
yet seen, a great wide window opening over the river and a round arched door
leading to the thatched hall. [*Drawing*.] A very bad drawing but I am put out
by having the object in front of me, "nature puts me out." There is a stone

floor and a stone-roofed entrance-hall with the door to winding stair to left, and then a larger thatched hall, beyond which is a cottage and kitchen. In the thatched hall imagine a great copper hanging lantern (which is, however, not there yet but will be I hope, next week). I am writing at a great trestle table which George keeps covered with wild flowers.[22]

The winter of 1919 was spent in England, and early in 1920 Yeats went on a lecture tour to America and had thoughts of going on with his wife to Japan, but decided against this. He paid a visit to Coole Park before going to England for the winter. The troubled state of Ireland prolonged the absence from Ballylee, but the desire to return is evident in the letters written at this time. During the winter of 1921 Yeats decided to obtain a house in Dublin and his wife went over and bought 82 Merrion Square. She went on to Ballylee to find that the builders had completed two more apartments in the castle. The recognition of Yeats by the leaders of the 'new Ireland' also encouraged his early return so that, despite the civil war in Ireland, the family were established at Ballylee in April 1922 and Yeats, who was then working on his memoirs, gave a name to his tower. A letter written to Olivia Shakespear in April says:

We are settled here now and our tower much near[er] finishing so that we have a large bed-room with a fine wooden ceiling, but it will be another year, so little labour is there to be got even if our money permitted, before we shall be complete. George is very happy to be back here and declares that the children have at once increased in weight. As I have not seen a paper for days I do not know how far we have plunged into civil war but it will hardly disturb us here. . . . What do you think of our address — Thoor Ballylee? Thoor is Irish for tower and it will keep people from suspecting us of modern gothic and a deer park. I think the harsh sound of "Thoor" amends the softness of the rest.[23]

In May, George was 'painting the bedroom ceiling in blue and black and gold'[24] and despite the troubled times in the country, life at the castle was delightful. On 5 June Yeats wrote to John Quinn:

Our bedroom is upstairs in the Castle and is a delight to us, and the third floor which is to be my study is almost ready. Our dining room on the ground floor was finished three years ago. This is the first year in which we have been able to sleep in the Castle itself. We have added an extra cottage, which is ultimately to be a garage, though not for anything nobler than a Ford. . . . None of these improvements has cost much. The stone for the cottage was dug out of the garden and the slates were bought two years ago for the Castle, which has to be concreted over instead, for our builder declares that no slate would withstand the storms. I went on my last American tour from Ballylee and that money is not all gone yet. It is a great pleasure to live in a place where George makes at every moment a fourteenth century picture. And out of doors, with the hawthorn all in blossom all along the river banks, everything is so beautiful that to go elsewhere is to leave beauty behind.[25]

8. Thoor Ballylee: The bedroom, 1926.

A collie puppy, cage-birds, the cottage, roofed in 'sea-green slates,' which was to become a garage are all mentioned in the letters of this summer as the work continued towards the completion of the building. A letter written on 7 June to Olivia Shakespear has:

Stone stairs to my surprise are the most silent of all stairs and sitting as I am now upstairs in the Tower I have a sense of solitude and silence. As yet we have no stranger's room, mainly because there is so little labour to be had. It will be the room above this, a beautiful room high in the tower. It is ready but for furniture and door.[26]

Another letter, to H. J. C. Grierson, dated 7 June has:

I am writing in my bedroom which is also, for the most part, my study; it is on the first floor of the Tower, there is an open fire of turf, and a great elm-wood bed made with great skill by a neighbouring carpenter, but designed by that late drunken genius Scott; and over my head is a wooden ceiling made according to his design. Some day it will be painted in brilliant colours. And the window is full of canaries, they and their nests, in a huge cage.[27]

The top room at the Tower remained unfinished and empty. Yeats had planned it as the scene of his spiritual meditations and hoped to finish *A Vision* there, at the top of the winding stair. Neither plan was realised. But the troubled time continued and a letter of 9 August to Herbert Palmer has this footnote:

I would ask you to call and see me but I live in a mediaeval tower on the West of Ireland, beside a bridge that may be blown up any night; and it may be a long time before I am in London.[28]

9. Thoor Ballylee: The living room, 1926.

10. Thoor Ballylee:
Fireplace in the
living room, 1926.

And in a letter of 18 August to T. Sturge Moore, Yeats says:

I am at Ballylee but get back to Dublin by August 24th. Little harm has been done here, despite rumours in the press, and even in the neighbouring towns, except the windows and doors burst in and various traces of occupation by Irregulars, stray bullets, signs that a bed has been slept in and so on. The Irregulars took care of our property and even moved a Russian icon of my wife's from a dry wall to a dry shelf, but after they had gone the country people stole all the mirrors. They left the blankets and such humdrum property but evidently found a novelty not to be resisted in the large mirrors.[29]

The bridge was in fact blown up, and a visit to see to the remaining works at the Tower postponed as the builder was shot and in hospital. Election to the Senate in November 1922, followed by the award of the Nobel Prize for Literature in 1923, left Yeats little time to pursue his idyllic life at Ballylee. He wrote to John Quinn on 29 January 1924 that 'Its chief use for some time to come will be to house the children, my wife and I going down for a few days at a time.'[30] The furnishing of Merrion Square and the support of the Cuala Press were large expenses and no lengthy stay was made at Ballylee until 1926. It was described in a letter to Olivia Shakespear on 25 May as 'this blessed place' where nothing happens 'but a stray beggar or a heron.'[31] The poems which were to form the volume entitled *The Tower* had been inspired by the mood of the place and T. Sturge Moore was asked to represent Thoor Ballylee in his binding for the book, which was published in 1928.

In *The Tower* Yeats had expressed the thought that this place was in a way a monument as well as a symbol. Ill-health dictated that the time spent there was coming to an end and his correspondence with Sturge Moore about the cover design for the book indicates his concern. He wrote to Sturge Moore on 23 May 1927:

I want you to design the cover — design in gold — and a frontispiece. The book is to be called *The Tower*, as a number of the poems were written at and about Ballylee Castle. The frontispiece I want is a drawing of the castle, something of the nature of a woodcut. If you consent I will send you a bundle of photographs. It is a most impressive building and what I want is an imaginative impression. Do what you want with cloud and bird, day and night, but leave the great walls as they are.[32]

Sturge Moore replied on 24 May that he would be glad to design the cover and had produced a sketch by the end of the month which Yeats returned on 2 June with the comment: 'It is interesting that you should have completed the Tower symbolism by surrounding it with water.'[33] In September, when the final drawings were in hand, Yeats wrote that

11. Cover design by T. Sturge Moore for *The Tower*, 1928.

the Tower should not be too unlike the real object, or rather that it should suggest the real object. I like to think of that building as a permanent symbol of my work plainly visible to the passer-by. As you know, all my art theories depend on just this — rooting of mythology in the earth.[34]

Ill-health took Yeats abroad in the winter of 1927 and he was in Rapallo when the book appeared on 14 February 1928. Sturge Moore's design was stamped in gold on olive green cloth and shows the tower reflected in water. Yeats wrote to him on 23 February:

Your cover for *The Tower* is a most rich, grave and beautiful design, admirably like the place, and I am all the more grateful because I may see but little of that place henceforth.[35]

By 1928 Yeats's use for the Tower had ended. He did not visit it again. The concerns which had informed the phase of his life connected with Thoor Ballylee had ceased to be relevant and he moved towards other accomplishments during his final ten years.

The death of Lady Gregory in May 1932 severed another link with Ballylee and the castle settled into the decline which was foreseen in the final version of the poem 'To be carved on a stone at Thoor Ballylee':

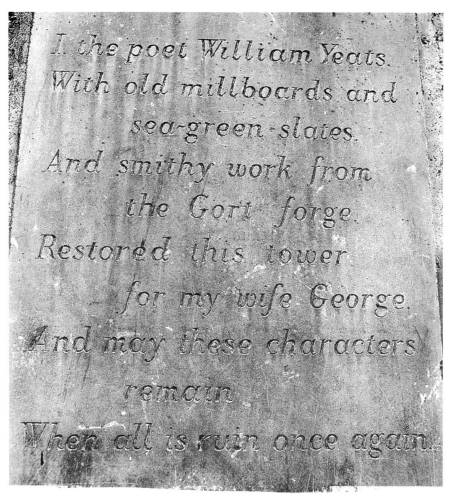

I the poet William Yeats.
With old millboards and
sea-green slates.
And smithy work from
the Gort forge.
Restored this tower
for my wife George.
And may these characters
remain
When all is ruin once again.

12. The inscription carved at Thoor Ballylee.

The stone with Yeats's inscription was not erected in his lifetime and had to wait until it was set up in 1948 by the board of the Abbey Theatre, who appointed Mr. Michael Scott as architect. The stone was designed by Mr. Pat. Scott and carved by the Dublin firm of Harrison & Sons Ltd. By this time the castle and cottages were rapidly falling into decay. Miss Virginia Moore visited the Tower in 1952 and wrote of it in her book *The Unicorn*:

Today the Norman tower at Ballylee is a barn for cattle and a rallying place for crows. ("That's the way we found it," said Mrs. Yeats when I reported the condition. "It's come full cycle.") But anyone who, like me, has stared at the circling river, ruined cottages, ancient appropriate mask on the tower's outer wall, and arched door, and then picked a path across manure in a splendid ground room, and, after unloading rocks barring the way, mounted the famous narrow winding stair with walls painted a piercing blue to examine the three higher apartments, piled up like blocks, noting the fine fireplace in one and the noble vaulted ceiling in another, and slit-windows, and little secret room, and looked out from the walled roof in sunlight over gently rolling Irish fields — anyone who has done this understands perfectly well what drew Yeats to Thoor Ballylee. No matter if the heavy oaken furniture, the thatch, rose garden, and bridge are gone.[36]

And in the introduction by D. J. Gordon and Ian Fletcher to the section 'Persons and Places' in the catalogue of the exhibition shown in Manchester and Dublin in 1961, *Images of a Poet*, they recorded:

The ruin has been accomplished with an almost too dramatic appropriateness; the cottage is now roofless; the garden overgrown with huge weeds; the tower roof leaks; graffiti are scribbled on the wall and window embrasure; rooms have been stripped of woodwork, and a plank has even been torn from the great oak door.

Ownership of Thoor Ballylee remained with the family of the poet.

*

13. W. B. Yeats and his children at Ballylee, 1926.

14. The thatching of the cottage, 1964.

The Kiltartan Society was founded by Mrs. Mary Hanley in 1961, and at its first meeting, held at Coole Park on 18 June of that year, the aims of the Society were proposed. Among these aims was the express purpose of the Society to foster interest in the literary history of the district and especially in the work of Yeats, Lady Gregory and Edward Martyn. The restoration of Thoor Ballylee was one of the principal objectives of the Society. Bord Fáilte (the Irish Tourist Board) had for some years been investigating the possibility of restoring the Tower and welcomed the co-operation and advice of the newly formed Society. Funds were provided by Bord Fáilte for the work of restoration. Mrs. Yeats and the poet's children, Michael and Anne, gave their full approval to the scheme and, in 1963, placed the property in the hands of a Trust formed to ensure its restoration and maintenance.

The architect chosen by Bord Fáilte for the reconstruction was Mr. Dermot O'Toole of Dublin and on the basis of his survey and researches plans were drawn up and the work put in hand. Later, the original drawings prepared by Professor Scott for Yeats were located and these, with a group of photographs taken by Thomas Hynes on a visit to Ballylee in 1926, which were presented to Mrs.

Hanley by Miss Mary Hynes of Dungory, Kinvara, made it possible to restore the original furnishings. Some of the original pieces were located in the district and others made by a local craftsman, Mr. Thomas Hyland. The walls were repainted in the original colours and the cottage was completely re-roofed in the traditional method and thatched by Mr. Paddy Lally of Peterswell near Ballylee. The reconstruction work was carried out by a local contractor, Mr. Maxie McDonnell, following in the tradition of Rafferty, who executed the original work for Yeats.

The restored Thoor Ballylee was declared open by Padraic Colum on Sunday, 20 June 1965, the Centenary Year of the poet's birth, and stands today as a lasting monument to William Butler Yeats, visited by thousands each year. Yeats's 'narrow winding stair' guides the visitor to the roof from which he can look north to Edward Martyn's Tulira or west to the seven woods which once enclosed Lady Gregory's house at Coole, now, by historic fate, a ruin where, in the overgrown garden, the great copper beech still bears in its bark, among those of many figures of the Irish Renaissance, the initials of W.B.Y.

15. Thoor Ballylee, from the vegetable garden, c. 1926.

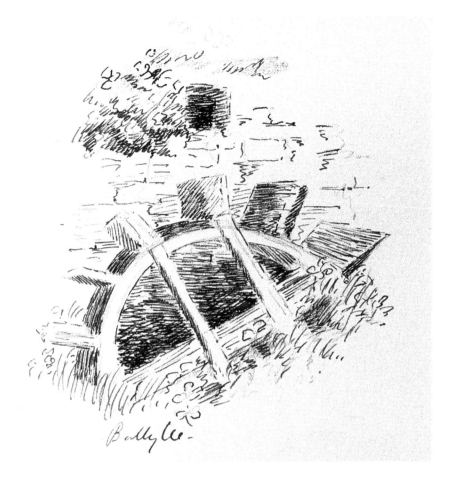

Ballyl__

16. Sketches by Lady Gregory, 14 August 1895.

Notes

Foreword

1　*CP* 230-31
2　'Upon a House Shaken by the Land Agitation.' *CP* 106

NOTES

The following abbreviations are used in referring to standard editions of Yeats's works : *L* for *The Letters of W. B. Yeats* edited by Allan Wade (London, 1954); *CP* for *The Collected Poems of W. B. Yeats* (London, 1950).

Thoor Ballylee

1　*CP* 227
2　'The Tower.' *CP* 221
3　'An Irish Airman foresees his Death.' *CP* 152
4　'Dust hath closed Helen's eye.' *Mythologies* 22
5　'Raftery's praise of Mary Hynes' in *The Kiltartan Poetry Book* by Lady Gregory (The Cuala Press, Dublin, 1918), 6
6　*L* 615
7　*L* 624
8　*L* 625
9　*L* 627
10　*Ibid.*
11　*L* 628
12　*L* 630
13　*L* 634
14　*L* 634
15　*L* 647
16　*L* 651
17　*L* 652
18　*CP* 148
19　*CP* 183
20　*CP* 226-27
21　*L* 659
22　Quoted in *W. B. Yeats* by Joseph Hone, 319
23　*L* 680
24　*L* 682
25　*L* 682-83
26　*L* 686
27　*L* 687
28　*L* 689
29　*W. B. Yeats and T. Sturge Moore. Their Correspondence 1901-1937*, ed. Ursula Bridge (London, 1953), 48
30　*L* 703
31　*L* 715
32　*Yeats/Sturge Moore Correspondence*, 109
33　*Ibid.*, 111
34　*Ibid.*, 114
35　*Ibid.*, 123
36　*The Unicorn* (London, 1954), 282

Acknowledgements

The first version of this essay originated in a paper delivered at Coole Park on 19 June 1961 by Mrs. Mary Hanley, founder of The Kiltartan Society. Her encouragement and assistance in preparing a text and in providing photographs is greatly appreciated. Acknowledgement is also made to Senator Michael Butler Yeats and Miss Anne Yeats for permission to quote from the writings of W. B. Yeats; and to the publishers of the following works which are quoted in the text:

The Collected Poems of W. B. Yeats (London, Macmillan, 1950).

Mythologies by W. B. Yeats (London, Macmillan, 1959).

The Letters of W. B. Yeats, edited by Allan Wade (London, Rupert Hart-Davis, 1954).

W. B. Yeats and T. Sturge Moore. Their Correspondence 1901-1937, edited by Ursula Bridge (London, Routledge & Kegan Paul, 1953).

W. B. Yeats by Joseph Hone (Second Edition, London, Macmillan 1962).

The Unicorn. W. B. Yeats's Search for Reality by Virginia Moore (London, Macmillan, 1954).

W. B. Yeats. Images of a Poet. Catalogue of an Exhibition held in Manchester and Dublin, compiled by D. J. Gordon and Ian Fletcher (Dublin, An Chomhairle Ealaíon, 1961).

LIAM MILLER